Praise for Yuyutsu RD Sharma

Yuyutsu's subject is the intertwinement of the social and geographic, namely, how even the Himalayas were dirtied and damaged by partisan politics. In the poems, sacred energy appears in sexual, rather than theological, form; his incredibly tangy descriptions of crags and cliff faces swell with eroticism.
Jim Feast in *The Brooklyn Rail*, New York

Each poem is a delight in itself, a discovery, a new turn of phrase, a new sensation, a world of sound and light, and visions all colliding against each other to provide an unexpected and haunting experience.
David Clark in *Exiled Ink*, London

Yuyutsu RD lives close to Everest. His poetry climbs mountains, swims in rivers, and paints the falling leaves in copper. This tango with nature also occurs when Yuyutsu RD closes the window for a moment...
Ronny Someck in *Iton77*, Tel Aviv

The poems... are shining jewels of passion, energy and splendid craft, redolent with vivid, dreamlike visual imagery, strengthened by realistic observation and powered by strong male eroticism. His is an unabashed return to the male gaze that is refreshing and solemn by turns, reminding one of the stirring sounds of rolling drums, and beating rain...
Sucheta Das Gupta in *The Himalayan Times*, Kathmandu

A fiercely sublime poet ...the book confirms an enormous talent, as well as purity of purpose with which he approaches his calling. Lines jump out, burning themselves into your consciousness.
Eddie Woods in *Amsterdam Weekly*

With this buoyantly audacious work, Yuyutsu RD should be assured of his place in the canon of Asian poetry.
In this new volume, he conveys the people and places, the flora and fauna of the Annapurna area of Nepal with an exhilaratingly fresh vision. It is poetry where pastoral elegy becomes fused with magic realism; where earthy common-sense mysticism becomes interlaced with a lush sexuality. The book is a voluptuous and loving evocation of Nepal and I admire its dramatic intensity.
Cathal O Searcaigh, Ireland

Yuyutsu RD Sharma's poetry runs clear, tender, and passionate with a rage that often erupts volcanic in the face of the cruelty, despair, and injustice that saddles the disenfranchised poor of the earth. Poems powerful and devastating, yet gentle as flower petals wafting to earth in a summer breeze.
Michael Annis, senior editor, *Howling Dog Press*, Colorado

This is what ***Asiaweek*** *has to say of* ***Yuyutsu's translations of Nepali poetry:***
'... magnificent achievement evoking lives of Nepalese peasants while remaining highly readable... The reader will come away breathless from these short, wonderfully concentrated poems'

These vivid and readable translations show the poets coming to terms both with political development and with the influence of Western modernism in literature.
-— **Allen W. Thrasher,**
Library of Congress, Washington DC

Young, versatile energetic, he is rocking and rolling with new impressions... Yuyutsu's poetry touches on concerns of global matters, acknowledging that we can never with violence create a Utopia or "construct a gorgeous pagoda from/furious flames/and whistling winds ... Such lines capture for me the futility of the Iraq War, which I refuse to dignify with its official title, even more euphemistic and tainted with doublethink than earlier misadventures. We can't build even a humble pagoda from furious flames and whistling winds.
— **David Ray,** The United States of America

"Yuyutsu R.D. brings to the Indian readers a distinct flavor of the Nepalese landscape and culture, in a sequence of poems that pulsate with needle-sharp images—Equally sensitive is his language that, scrupulously avoids stilted diction-words or phrases. His writing is so densely imagistic that he holds reader's attention all the way through. Behind plethora of packed images is a genuine concern for the human predicament the trials and tribulations of the destitute everywhere. Hunger is the theme that runs as an under current-hunger that gnaws into the vitals of both humans and animals."
—**Shiv K. Kumar** in ***The Hindustan Times***

"Something is always happening in Yuyutsu's poetry. Like some burning concern for truth, something that, I think, a poem should do. For this, we owe Yuyutsu much.
— **Jayanta Mahapatra,** Cuttack, India

Yuyutsu has a good eye and a good ear:
The rain stopped in the jungle.
The cicada stopped its chirr.
To have an ear for a sudden silence in unique.
— **Keki N. Daruwala** in *The Hindustan Times*

"Yuyutsu's poetry has long been a part of the Nepalese consciousness: We use his more aphoristic lines as a paradigm of contemporary Nepali political and social changes."
—The Kathmandu Post

Some Female Yeti is a tribute to the various changing as well as timeless aspects of the Himalayan Kingdom. There is crippling

touch of stark and naked reality in these poems. They remind us of the time when women were raped, men were killed and human rights were abused. Yes, some of the poems deal with the democratic upsurge and its aftermath in Nepal."
— *Connection*

"It is an agony ride through the darkness of modern times. The symbols are powerful and disturbing, the metaphors violent. The female Yeti becomes as icon for man's sexual angst... This collection marks an important phase in the poet's evolution, revealing a more mature poet in terms of symbol, diction and style. 'Hitting notes of a secret language of lust', Yuyutsu has made his poetic presence felt."
—*The Observer*

"...Highly vibrant portrayal of the individual's existential issues, ranging from the mundane deprivations to the primordial lust and passion, anguish and anger... Equally powerful is the author's projection of the public life in all its shenanigans, conspiracies and treachery.
The most redeeming aspect of Yuyutsu's poetry is his powerful writing style that brings forth the human experience directly without the binds of sophistication that tends to dissipated original spirit. The rawness of his writing is so exhilarating; it brings the full flavor of the locale to the sense."
—*The Rising Nepal*

Yuyutsu's poetry is the poetry of agony and anger. It does not soothe; it shocks. It does not lull; it awakens the reader to a reality he is least bothered about. Also, it has a distinct native flavor: maize fields, bare cots, hearths, querns, mud-plastered wall, and a grain of monsoon. It is different from the poetry of those who roll in the labyrinth of inner life or rejoice in the cities where skyscrapers bloom. His poetry is evidently akin to the regional literatures he is familiar with, Punjabi, Hindi and Nepali.
— *The Indian Literature*

In Yuyutsu R.D.'s poems you can feel nature — the rainbow, the river, the day and night. Nature is a metaphor to express human agony and Yuyutsu draws this situation in strong and rich colors. In his poems about poetry, Yuyutsu metaphors are galloping, noble and wild. He shows us other specials ways we need in the face of poetry.
— **Ronny Someck,** Israel

Nirala Series

HUNGER OF OUR HUDDLED HUTS

Recipient of fellowships and grants from The Rockefeller Foundation, Ireland Literature Exchange, The Institute for the Translation of Hebrew Literature and The Foundation for the Production and Translation of Dutch Literature, **Yuyutsu RD Sharma** is a distinguished poet and translator. He has published seven poetry collections, including, *Annapurna Poems,* (Nirala, New Delhi 2008), *Everest Failures* (White Lotus Book Shop, Kathmandu, 2008) *www.WayToEverest.de: A photographic and Poetic Journey to the Foot of Everest,* (Epsilonmedia, Germany, 2006) with German photographer Andreas Stimm and a translation of Irish poet Cathal O' Searcaigh poetry in Nepali in a bilingual collection entitled, *Kathmandu: Poems: Selected and New,* 2006. He has translated and edited several anthologies of contemporary Nepali poetry in English and launched a literary movement, Kathya Kayakalpa (Content Metamorphosis) in Nepali poetry.

Widely traveled author, he has read his works at several prestigious places including Poetry Café, London, Seamus Heaney Center for Poetry, Belfast, Western Writers' Center, Galway, Bowery Poetry Place, New York, Knox College, Illinois, Whittier College, California, Baruch College, New York, WB Yeats' Center, Sligo, Gustav Stressemann Institute, Bonn, Rubin Museum, New York, Irish Writers' Centre, Dublin, The Guardian Newsroom, London, Arnofini, Bristol, Borders, London, Royal Society of Dramatic Arts, London, Gunter Grass House, Bremen, GTZ, Kathmandu, Ruigoord, Amsterdam, Nehru Center, London, Frankfurt Book Fair, Frankfurt, Indian International Center, New Delhi, and Villa Serbelloni, Italy. He has held workshop in creative writing and translation at Queen's University, Belfast, and South Asian Institute, Heidelberg University, Germany.

His works have appeared in *Poetry Review, Chanrdrabhaga, Sodobnost, Amsterdam Weekly, Indian Literature, Irish Pages, Omega, Howling Dog Press, Exiled Ink, Iton77, Little Magazine, The Telegraph, Indian Express* and *Asiaweek.*

Born at Nakodar, Punjab and educated at Baring Union Christian College, Batala and later at Rajasthan University, Jaipur, Yuyutsu remained active in the literary circles of Rajasthan and acted in plays by Shakespeare, Bertolt Brecht, Harold Pinter, and Edward Albee. Later he taught at various campuses of Punjab University, and Tribhuwan University, Kathmandu.

The Library of Congress has nominated his recent book of Nepali translations entitled *Roaring Recitals; Five Nepali Poets* as Best Book of the Year 2001 from Asia under the Program, A World of Books International Perspectives.

Yuyutsu's own work has been translated into German, French, Italian, Slovenian, Hebrew, Spanish and Dutch. Currently on a North American tour, he edits *Pratik, A Magazine of Contemporary Writing* and contributes literary columns to Nepal's leading daily, *The Himalayan Times* and *Newsfront Weekly*. He has completed his first novel.

More: www.yuyutsu.de

Hunger of our Huddled Huts

& Other Poems

Yuyutsu RD Sharma

Nirala

Nirala Publications
G.P.O. Box 7004
Daryaganj, New Delhi-110002
niralabooks@yahoo.co.in
www.niralapublications.com

First Edition 1998
Second Editon 2011

ISBN-81-8250-010-9

Cover Illustration: Yuyutsu RD Sharma

Cover Design: S.A.A. Wasti

Printed at
H.S. Offset Printers
New Delhi-11000

Contents

CRONE'S CORPSE

For
fellow travelers

MILKY OCEAN OF GENEROSITY

Wrath

The clouds can
blind the valley, what can
the fat Moon do.
But ardent raindrops
bring in their own music
and thus
I hear stones speak
leaves sing
and the brook's tumultuous whistle
and then
the sky cracks open
with a blast
and the thatched roofs
crumble over the praying people.

Fate

Monsoon cicadas
shriek shrill...
The old dog
dozing beside a goitered
drunken porter huddled
under a pagoda temple's
huge brassy bell
would wake up
if only some gorilla
kick crushes his pus dripping paw.

From the Kulekhani Tunnels

Meeting those
who serve
those who suffer
seems sufficient.
This witch-
girl's sagged
breast hanging
out of her frail
blouse is diseased
like a cur's
rotten ear,
has been sucked
madly dry
by those whose
mouths are ulcerous.
Of course,
the monkey babe
clinging
to her decaying
lump of flesh
is an utter fool,
is sucking pus.
In the smoke
strangled tea
shacks yellow
helmets numbered
in crab legged

Japanese letters
dangle languid,
telling how
in the blind
interiors nightshifts
and daylights
share throes
of dust grains
in the life's
bleeding eye.

Wounds that bleed

In Bhimphedi
they would celebrate an overcast
dusty December noon.
The yellow locust
skittering triumphant
through the furling stalks
of the golden grass.
"Can't sit before
our cracking hearth, can't!
O wretched low caste,
don't you moan like a bitch.
Take your vaginal
 wounds away!
Aren't you listening? Don't you
moan like a bitch,
an ulcerous, ill-omened bitch!"
Even this little boy
from her own village
wouldn't help her. See, see
his own cheeks burn bright,
has been slapped
repeatedly by the landlady
for being friendly
with dogs and urchins.
Enraged instead,
he blasts note of dread.
"Why would you sit

in here like a Brahmin?
Can't you go away?
why unmindful of
the curse of god...."
He stops,
rubs his eyes in smoke,
an awkward Copperfield,
figuring finales
of fate, then resolves
"Yeah, that's why,
that's why your womb
bleeds, that's why
the wounds
of your womb bleed!"

Set

1

Sahu's fat
rooster strolling in the main square

issues
a careless crow.

A five-year-old
hillside son enters the valley,

barely clad,
barefoot, holding his bee

bitten hand
up in the blue sky

as if
it were a trophy,

his innocent
hand swollen and wavering

like a cobra's
hideous fang

2.

Snake stung
swollen ankle

on Bhimphedi's
main square he exhibits,

the valorous
son of suffering.

Swollen-eyed
slow saviors scrutinize

the sorry scene.

The Fall

Sunlight
flushes forth,

it's morning,
a beginning winter morn.

Roosters crowing,
bleak without visions

of smoke curls
rising skywards.

Querns languishing,
hungry to glimpse golden silos of plenty.

But the fatal weight
of the bulky nose rings

tempers
their potential for screams.

Tragic featured
girls go into dry jungles.

Thorns blaze on the hill paths
to kiss their maiden footsteps.

A bush
of wounds bursts forth

into a scarlet flames
to fight back the agents of the Fall.

Milky Ocean of Generosity

Sahuni passing
through a bout of her summer menstruation

in the dark cabin
of a tea shack issues violent snorts.

Outside, a squashy
hillside Sun suddenly changes color and growls

to scorch the valley
of winter, deepening distances.

The oak tree spread over
the shack whistles at intervals, swished wind slaps.

The streets humming languorous,
peopleless except the inert patches

of fetid curs asleep
near the cries of dusty kids.

Who is here to stop
the ferocious honey bees pestering the aged servant

carrying a huge cauldron
of pure buff milk to the crackling hearth?

You think he knows
what his crying face of a dying baboon looks like?

Smoke stifles him
and the crystal tears drip

into her milky ocean of generosity.

Ulcers of Poverty

Didn't you suck
the juice of our helpless bodies?

Didn't you render
us pallid as the patches of hay

drying in the crotches
of the bare branched December trees?

Grandson of our corrupt heroes

can you too blame snow storms,
lethal wind slaps or furious flood?

Can you too crush blossom
big bride of our village

and put blame
on Lord Shiva's invisible linga?

Dreamy drunk,
would you see romance

in the dance of the drunken deaf
drumming to soothe the soul

of a Lama babe
torn apart by the dogs of hunger

while the wandering woman
from Kokette crouches in the womb

of ferocious Kali, hearing the drums'
recurrent beats in her ulcers of poverty?

Screech

A sob wallowing
in the slimy throat of a dark pond dies.

Daggers of shimmering snow spear up,
singsong of summer cicadas get hushed.

Hungry devotees shuffle for embers
of survival in the conch shell city's slimy labyrinth.

Winter fogs come, fumbling furious
to silence jubilant life bells of the valley.

Sutras of the sacred scrolls
start issuing an ominous stench

a soon-to-be paralyzed hand
exploring a warm heap of buff's body

fails to
clean its babe's running nose.

A cry spirals fanwise
to unhinge joints of a hollowed house

as a bony figure doubles
ver a green pond's shattered spout

to light the dark
night of a makeshift heart

What more do you expect,
a frozen bucket of thick bestial blood?

Headpieces shatter against
the pillars of the bronze Lord

and endlessly wandering woman's
vulgar smile crashes into a screech.

BELLY & BELOW

On a bright cloudless day

The clouds gone
in the dawn. The jackals wail

in the valley, ill- ominous .
Large-hipped hill girl plasters

her hut's threshold
with cow dung. Inside, her sister

opens her dream stuck
legs for the bow- shaped Pa to stir

a furnace
full of rusting knives.

Her lanky brother
is taken into the hydro tunnel

by a Japanese Land rover.
The eldest sister returns home

loaded under
a flowery pile of grass.

Sahu's son waits
in the doorway, waiting her to plough

his land for a free lunch
on a bright cloudless day.

Failures

In the mud floored porch
of a misty little shack

by the raging brook's
soft edge, peeling

the skins
of maize off, aflush

amidst its fluffy pile
sits a hillside mother

with a son
wailing in her laps.

She has
nothing but a kiss,

a soily
soppy stinking kiss

to shut
this wailing kitten up.

Way of the Brook

Come down, clouds,
come hissing to smash the bowl of my passions.
The daughter of cataracts
opens a tea shack on a brook's bank.
The black tuft end of her braids
she keeps in her scarlet skirt's pocket.
The drivers from the Kulekhane project
gather at her glistening threshold, hauling out smiles.
Her right hand pours tea while
the other fumbles to hide the lucent
parting between her butter bright breasts.
Sunken cheeked baboons
firewood bundles unloaded nearly
squat around her crackling hearth
counting ulcers of their anxiety.
With the swish of her skirt, clouds,
come to cool the porches of their crumbling huts
smoldering on the seething breast of a dusty hilltop.

From the shoulder of ash green hills
come here. Follow me, clouds,
for I will show you your movements here,
her snowy finders quietly combing
the fragrant gardens of her gloom.
I will show you, clouds,
the construction of the hearth.
Young Kancha bringing sand pans

from the brook's bank where lilies
undress to sketch the motion of your dreams
Hungry human being munching beaten rice,
their hands smeared with sour curd,
almond eyed hill girls giggling at
the stork poise of a baboon
towering above the exhaustion
of a maize sack, breathless
on the stony plinth of her shop,
violent anguished curls of smoke rising
along the harsh outbursts of cough,
thundering speed of your lightning.
Clouds, I will show you
the wrinkled face of a toothless papa
crying over the body of a lamb
torn apart by the jackals of the blue jungle.

Come here, clouds,
to find this goitred Grandma
holding her grandson's corpse
wet from the gnawing anxiety of a coffin.
Come here, clouds,
to see this hunchbacked shepherdess
whistling to locate the lamb
lost somewhere in the curdled confusion of yours.

Hunger of our Huddled Huts

The rainstorm that
washes clammy beehives

dripping honey
in your cedar garden of tangled bear boughs

that eases anxiety
of your smoldering passion points

that churns your green
mountains into ethereal ejaculations

can only scratch
cheeks of our innocent wheat fields

can only race crazed
over the hunger of our huddled huts.

Crazed

Maria,
the roof of my brain glazes,
ten thousand serpents welded
together, throbbing......
Were the kisses taken
better than those you rejected?
But this frail fourteen years
old squint-eyed porter dozing
in the cold deluxe bus struggling
in the chilled valley rose
as if wounded in his sleep—
his reeking jaws clamped ,
his limbs fluttering anarchic,
and fell, a sullen sack
of insensate flesh on two pilgrims and
a grandma sleeping on the frozen bus floor.....
His mouth frothing,
his limbs curled like tender twigs
and the grandma buried
beneath the divine scourge, hollering....
Get me a shoe, please,
a shoe please. It's urgent, Maria,
it's urgent ! I want
to bring the boy back to senses.

Belly and Below

Dusty mule path's granite edges
crumble onto the luminous bed of the brook.
In the rain drenched pine forest
a bright-eyed curlew watches this,
ready to articulate a lusty screech,
waiting for the dark powers to possess
the sparkling scene. On huge mossy rocks
sunk in sands washed by brooks
some hungry jackals lie cuddled together,
edgily waiting to dig out
last night's buried lust for flesh.
In the tumultuous belly of the brook
what do these fragile legs
puffed from elephantiasis grope for?
Is it a bit of flesh to bestowed
by the benevolent lord? gauchely ransacking
the heart of a damp hole
above the wall blackening hearth?
Is it a match-box, a tin kerosene lamp
or a cake of detergent soap?
Last night, love, how many did feed
upon the shores of your flesh ?
At the gurgling river bank
why to wash your swollen sins?
Father, you know , can't catch flesh
in the ageing net. O Girlfriend of wounds,
can't you see the droplets of blood

dripping from the horizon's wounded breast?
Can't you hear the yellow hydro-electric jeeps
rattling down along the hissing brook?
The dust they stir almost
stifles the essence of the brook.
Why to wash your wounds right now?
Just notice that eyeless cicada
set in the green of the weeping willow
beside a deaf waterfall beginning
his nocturnal shrill of crazed carnality.

Rains

Even oriole's swinging nest
gets wet. Sun's powerful face flares
in your mind. The natives go to the brook's bank
to watch its speedy swell.
Torrential currents carry the crumbling
hill edges away to the Indian plains.
The passages get blocked. Below a leaking
waterdrum under a tea shack's rusting
edifice a deaf dog-eyed old servant
splashes his rotting hands spewing out
a river of hidden anger.
Isn't his pus that you are
eating like butter with your bread ?
Your heart thumps hysteric,
you throw your bread away which
wet chickens waddling with their woeful
mother peak at. Then a babe bursts
a pile of dirt by a cauldron
full of dead honeybees. The helping hens
desert the bread to clean the babe's mess up.
Enraged, you kick the foul smelling
dog dozing under your bench, sentencing him
to fester his sore ulcers
under the dripping sky of Bhimphedi.

Jewel

Rest, rest!
Perturbed sprit!
Groaning dog- faced sky!
Don't howl on the hilltops.
Don't stir the birds
mating in their cosy nests.
Mosquitoes have died.
Ah! wings,
flimsy wings broken
Chickens are dying,
and fragile- boned duckling too,
stumbling down
into dirty rills.
My stem-soft babe
lies asleep in the hut,
dreaming of his dead
mother's nipples
(She died vomiting blood).
My Lord, my master.
succulent blood
of tender lambs
I will offer you,
blood sweet as my babe's.
O, owner of my destiny,
don't shake the shack,
so fragile!....

My babe lies
curled up in the shack
as if in his Ma's womb.
O Tempestuous
O Mighty! Bhima's brother!
Shaker of the mountains!
Don't shriek,
don't tear
drops will drop
into his tiny ears.
Rest, rest,
perturbed sky
don't growl,
don't bring raindrops,
frost, fog, hail, skulls
in human hands.
O windy spirit
O mighty!
tic tic of his tiny
heart will die
a dream built
with a bird's effort.

Hero of the Hills

By the fiery hearth
a rain soaked hen fettered
for the forthcoming festival
is laid on the tea hut's mud floor.
At once a fat rooster flaps
amuck towards her, crazed
to clutch her wet body
to hit her head with his
jagged beak. In haste
he climbs over
and tilts backwards
to shoot a jolt from below.
A coarse hand slaps the rooster.
He swings onto
the squelching street, desperately
clutching at a tiny broom
of hen's feathers tight in his beak.
Before the crackling hearth's
mouth lies the panting hen,
turned upside down,
her excited womb
opening, closing, opening, closing,
undulating slaps of the summer rain.

The Heroine of the Hills

Her teeth chattering,
her eyes groggy,
bulging out, foggy.
On finding her ankles
stained with blood
she gets terrified...
She opens her trousers
hurriedly
and retches back
in horror,
a blood-spattered fist
open,
dangling
between her thighs
like a balloon
or a burst melon,
blood red and clear.
She finds
her accumulated
life-strength
seeping out through
her uterus.
The hovering hoof
of the huge black buffalo
crashed below her navel
like a colossal hammer
ah a fierce blow!

She shakes
and moans
revisiting the moment
of the bellowing buffalo
romping madly in the field
while she,
her trampled victim
lay alone
drenching in the field...
The uterus came out
slipped out
and dangled
an orphaned life
between her hefty thighs
wet with blood
dripping, dyeing
the white
of the hospital bench...

Raid

The shrunken bundle
of grandma's bones tapping

the frozen screens
the glistening Maruti vans

would fling up
in the blue of the valley

scattered
by a brutal kick.

The leper struggling
through the rush of the scurrying

pavement dwellers
gathering grains of their livelihood

would stop
to pick up a fat-leaved benediction

bowl lying triumphant
on the Lord's scarlet point.

The pavements would
get deserted for the fleshy skirts

and the clang
of the horse hoofs would die away.

Only that crazed woman
would remain, calling them names.

You wouldn't dare to
stare into big swollen eyes,

daggers of sunlight.

Holi

Spring comes late here.
The valley becomes an ash- tray,
a deserted studio of ghosts.
Straw strikes and straw survives.
Cataracts of fire tumble down
the dry hills. Even pines turn pale,
and cedars fade, and firs too,
and lie piled up
in the porches of the dying hunts.
The scarlet-flowered laligurans,
the drying survivor of the valley,
gives up the ghost. A capital of crickets,
cicadas, it's all locust grey,
grey, grey and sweeping blue above.
The crumbling huts flop down.
The pillars of the porches stumble
and then die. Dust rises,
drifts about in the heated sky,
then slowly settles down
on the collapsed pile of human endeavor.
A fading failing landscape,
fuel for the cataracts of fire,
fuel for lonely lovers lost for a lifetime.

Holi, festival of colours.
The drunks dance and die drinking local wine.

Yes, the colors,
the last night's colors
still stay in her hair,
in the creases of her eyelids,
in the cute nostrils,
in the porches of her ears.
Playing colours games is easy,
making bodies dazzle bright difficult.

Ah! the blotched walls ,
the spotted wooden doors of the wine shops,
of the tea -shacks,
the splattered threshold of her house,
her flushed face!

Sun flares up bright,
the luxuriance of the colors dies.
Time for baboons to come
from the neighbouring hillsides,
bundles of firewood on their backs,
clad in semi- dark slimy rags.
What's it the keeps
their swollen eyes aglitter?
Muscular, nerves -puffed,
they shuffle past (sturdy stalks!)
lost in the blackout of their lives,
uninterrupted, knowing
this world of Bhimphedi isn't theirs,

knowing their sun lies ashamed
under the silent querns of their barren huts
confident of not going to be assaulted
with the uproar of festivity.

Range

The burden
of the nightshift's filth

the bare bargain
of blue dawns and emerald hill ranges

for bleeding eyes
of dark tunnels

of spinach piles pots
of curd jerkins of fresh milk

for beds
of liquor vomits

and a lifetime's
sickness in a drowse

that's death.

CRONE'S CORPSE

Rajasthan

In the fragile
shade of a shrub

two camels
sit, chewing cud

issuing
forth froth

watching
the blistering white of the sky

not a grain
of the Monsoons.

The 1984 Assassination: Jaipur

The scarlet point
of the angry Sun drops

behind the Albert Museum.
Pigeons come, dropping dirt

on the rose hewn domes.
In the tiled courtyard

of the SMS Hospital
scarlet turbaned patients lie

waiting for a dog end.
A large hermaphrodite limps

among them, exposing
one of his ugly breasts.

In the general ward
malnourished housewives swarm

around the stiff steel
tables of spectacled Dr. Guptas.

In the neon lights
of the festering pavements

weak bats lie, not knowing
the children in their laps

have moved out
to the other world.

The betel chewing vultures
strut below bright Bollywood posters,

their stunned faces
lit by the theater's lucent lights.

The Guest of Gunti

Ramanand Rathi's
house on the hill
top in the heart
of the blazing desert
plains. The mother lies
smothered in blind
bleak rooms with
clay plastered walls.
As you take your
shower in the open
courtyard, the mother
upstairs in the smoke-filled
kitchen stirs flames
in her humble hearth.
Later in the white-
washed porch
you lie, roof built
with tangled boughs
of an oak tree, lie
on the bare cot
caught in a watery
drowse listening
to the squeaking
herons and abrupt
chorus of peacocks
opening in the fields
far off, reading Turgnev

and Gogol in his absence.
The dust-smeared
children and elders
gather in the street
gazing in at you
as if you come
from the other world,
envious of not having
a guest. The mother
ruffles your hair
with love, your head
pressed against her bosom,
thanking the urchins who
brought you home
safe, saving her precious
guest from violent cats
and scavenging
stray dogs of Gunti.

Crash

Across the dark
green spring
fields of Gunti
where jewel
necked blue peacocks
peck shade under
the glossy peepal
burns the corpse.
"Died last night,"
tells the young boy,
"as the thundering storm
struck her fragile hut.
I knew it beforehand,
Didn't you notice
gods weep
in the dead of the night..."
The buffets of the wind
banged brutally
her door opened
with a bang.
The slimy weight fell
on her famished frame
and thus she collapsed.
dared to answer
Time's fatal call?
Dust floating
in the cringing corners..

"Only last year,"
he continues,
"her young daughter
took her life,
the landlord's son
tried to straighten his..."
Rope of self- immolation.
"That very year
her blind husband passed away,
tuberculosis you know..."
He walks besides
the yellow flowered
field on the fragrant passage,
narrating a family's
heroic annihilation,
his nostrils quivering
from the overwhelming
fragrance of the greenery,
his uncouth hand crushing
a tiny yellow mustard
flower, a complete
world in itself

Curls

The mother's breaking
dry firewood in
the doorless kitchen upstairs.
See the curls of smoke
rise skywards,
see the tiny clouds of dust too
floating in the sky and
then slowly settling
upon cat's glossy back.
She's making
a cup of tea for her guest.
Sit on the bare cot
watching urchins'
effort to irritate her cat
by making faces,
by goggling eyes.
Sit on the bare cot
to watch your mother
bring water from the wells.
see the Sun stooping over
barren Araveli hill ranges.
Sleep now,
can't step out of the main door.
Just yesterday
a boy died, how villainous
those low caste boys!
No, can't even stroll outdoors.

Shadows getting longer,
bright fields fading
under the cover of the dark.
Can't you hear
stray dogs of Gunti weep
and whine in the cold moonlit night?
Can't you feel the drunks
of the village shout abuses
in the narrow streets?
My pearl, my son,
sleep inside with
our curly tailed cat
(as he herself sleeps
in the doorless December
kitchen upstairs)
waiting for
of the morning glory.

Ma Dreams

"Get a job now, son,
got to build our house.
Get me a bride too,
one for you
and one for your brother."

Pouring hot tea
on the stale crumbs
in the Chinese bowl
for her cat, throwing
abuses at the intruding
dogs, the mother speaks.
Her words fall softly
on the feverish bottom
of my sinking heart.
"Got to build a brick house.
Can't work anymore,
lying on life's threshold,
waiting for the dark
word to drop
from the heavens...
Can't bring water
from the distant wells.
Can't carry heavy
water pots. Last time,
I fainted near the well,
fell flat in the slimy ditch

beside the water well...
aging you know!

Get a job now,
get me a bride too,
one for your brother
and one for you..."

The cat's lucent
tail curls in the air.

Urchin

"Ma repeatedly
warns us against
the stray dogs of Gunti,
especially against
the muscular, big-jawed
dog without a tail,
just a tag!
Hoh! What a tail..."
His narration
in his childish lisp,
his five-year-old
infected but big eyes
dancing bright...
dressed in a ragged coat
of much bigger size.
He'll sing songs
of village girls in love
if you offer a coin
and will follow you
to the village edge
where yellow fields begin...
"All other dogs
from Gunti are just fine
and friendly except
this black one.
Ma! he rushes on
swirling his bushy tail

to gobble you up.
No one can touch him,
what to talk of killing him.
No, the villagers won't
let anyone do it.
Even, Ma just warns us
to stay away from him,
to be careful...

Why can't we
kill the dog who bites?

Ruins

The anguish
of the dried up water wells fails

to patch up
the gaping cracks in the mud walls.

The peacock's thirsty cry
spreads its shuddering blaze

smashing sand pitchers
of the village virgins circling

the shrine in the Banyan tree's hollowed
trunk to get impregnated from a seed of some cooler god

Dusty storms curdle
the skies of her dreams

as the sandy wind slaps ruin
the taste of her brother's bread

on the bare
field's parched edge.

Your rolling in the cool
riverbed like a camel won't ease

the pang of his hunger's
fate in his bloodless veins.

The night hums to
the notes of shrieking peacocks and ominous owls

to console the desert
mother wailing by her son's feverish cot

struggling all night
to keep her hold on

the reins
his dying breath's regime.

Nirala Series

A Series of contemporary Writing

Annapurna & Stains of Blood
Life, travels Writing on a page of snow
Yuyutsu R D Sharma
ISBN 81-8250- 012-5 2009 Hard pp.200

Ocean in a Drop
Yoga, Meditation and Life in the Himalayas
Swami Chandresh
ISBN 81-8250- 005-2 2006 Hard pp.348

Maoists in the Land of Buddha
An Analytical Study of the Maoist Insurgency in Nepal
Prakash A. Raj
ISBN 81-85693-42-0 2004 Hard pp.210

The Yeti
Spirit of Himalayan Forest Shamans
Larry G. Peters
ISBN 81-85693-57-9 2004 Hard pp.128

Rana Rule in Nepal
Shaphalya Amatya
ISBN 81-85693-67-6 2004 Hard pp.408

Trance, Initiation & Psychotherapy in Nepalese Shamanism
Essays on Tamang and Tibetian Shamanism
Larry G.Peters
ISBN 81-85693-79-X 2004 Hard pp.412

Folk Tales of Sherpa and Yeti
Collected by Shiva Dhakal
Adapted by Yuyutsu RD Sharma
ISBN 81-8250-002-0 2009 Paper pp.125

The Gurkha Connection
A History of Gurkha Recruitment in the British Army
Purushottam Baskota
ISBN 81-85693-77-3 2006 Paper pp.221

Dolpo :The Hidden Paradise
A Journey to the Endangered Sanctuary of the Himalayan Kingdom of Nepal
Karna Sakya
ISBN 81-85693-73-0 2006 Paper pp.246

Malla Coins of Medieval Nepal
Jagdish Chandra Regmi
ISBN 81-85693-60-9 2008 Hard

The Dhimals: Miraculous Migrants of Himal
An Anthropological Study of a Nepalese Ethnic Group
Rishikeshab Raj Regmi
ISBN 81-8250-009-7 1991 Hard pp.269

The Questions of Dharma in the Mahabhatara
Birendra Mishra
ISBN 81-85693-48-X 2007 Hard pp.226

The Gurungs: Thunder of Himal
A Cross-Cultural Study of a Nepalese Ethnic Group
Murari P. Regmi
ISBN 81-85693-49-8 2002 Paper pp.238

The Gurkhas
A History of the Recruitment in the British Indian Army
Kamal Raj Singh Rathaur
ISBN 81-85693-85-4 2000 Paper pp.128

The Political Economy of Land, Landlessness and Migration in Nepal
Nanda R. Shrestha
ISBN 81-85693-87-0 2001 Hard pp.309

Tourism in Nepal
Marketing Challenges
Hari Prasad Shrestha
ISBN 81-85693-69-2 2000 Hard pp.399

Ethnic Conflict in Bhutan
Political and Economic Dimensions
Mathew Joseph C.
ISBN 81-85693-68-4 1999 Hard pp.251

Mountain Dimensions
An Altitude Geographic Analysis of Environment and Development of the Himalayas
Ram Kumar Pandey
ISBN 81-85693-43-9 1999 pp.260 Hard

Tamang Shamans
An Ethnopsychiatric Study of Ecstasy and Healing in Nepal
Larry G. Peters
ISBN 81-8250-009-5 2007 Paper pp.179

Wildlife in Nepal
Rishikesh Shaha & Richard M. Mitchell
With Color Plates by Nanda Shumsher J.B. Rana
ISBN 81-85693-31-5 2001 Paper pp.142

Nepal: Missing Elements in the Development Thinking
Gunanidhi Sharma
ISBN 81-85693-66-8 2000 Hard pp.282

Art and Culture of Nepal
An Attempt towards Preservation
Saphalya Amatya
ISBN 81-85693-63-3 1999 Hard pp.282

Recent Nepal
An Analysis of Recent Democratic Upsurge and its Aftermath
Laksman Bhadur K.C.
ISBN 81-85693-24-2 1993 Hard pp.242

Making of Modern Nepal
A Study of History, Art and Culture of the Principalities of Western Nepal
Ram Niwas Pandey
ISBN 81-85693-37-4 1997 Hard pp.816

Politics and Development in Nepal:
Some Issues
Narayan Khadka
ISBN 81-85693-21-8 1994 Hard pp.477

Indo-Nepal Trade Relations
A Historical Analysis of Nepal's Trade with the British India
Shri Ram Upadhyaya
ISBN 81-85693-20-X 1992 pp.287

Secrets of Shangri-La
An Inquiry into the Lore, Legend and Culture of Nepal
Nagendra Sharma
ISBN 81-85693-18-8 1992 pp.292

The Taming of Tibet
A Historical Account of Compromise and Confrontation
in Nepal-Tibet Relations (1900-1930)
Tirtha Prasad Mishra
ISBN 81-85693-16-1 1991 pp.324

Glimpses of Tourism, Airlines and Management in Nepal
B.R. Singh
ISBN 81-85693-15-3 1991 pp.128 Rs.125

Sales Promotion in Nepal
Policies and Practices
Parashar Prasad Koirala
ISBN 81-85693-14-5 1991 pp.196

Hindu-Buddhist Festival of Nepal
Hemant Kumar Jha
ISBN 81-85693-40-4 1996 Hard pp.117

Transit of Land Locked Countries and Nepal
Gajendra Mani Pradhan
ISBN 81-85693-08-0 1990 pp.240

Fundamentals of Library and Information Science
A Nepalese Response
Madhusudan Sharma Subedi
ISBN 81-85693-07-4 1990 pp.229

Folk Culture of Nepal
An Analytical Study
Ram Dayal Rakesh
ISBN 81-85693-06-4 1990 Hard pp.129

A Macro-economic Study of the Nepalese Plan Performance
Gunanidhi Sharma
ISBN 81-85693-06-4 1989 pp.129

Sources of Inflation in Asia
Theory and Evidences
Raghab D. Pant
ISBN 81-85693-03-X 1988 Hard pp.118

New Directions in Nepal- India Relations
Rishikesh Shaha
ISBN 81-85693-53-6 1995 Paper pp.59

LITERATURE

Annapurna Poems
Yuyutsu RD Sharma
ISBN 81-8250-013-5 2008 Hard pp.150

After Tagore
Poems Inspired by **Rabindranath Tagore**
David Ray
ISBN 81-8250-007-9 2007 Hard pp. 115

Kathmandu
Poems Selected and New (An English/Nepali Bilingual Edition)
Cathal O Searcaigh
Translated from the Gaelic by **Seamus Heaney, John Montague and others**
Translated into the Nepali by **Yuyutsu R.D. Sharma**
ISBN 81-8250-006-0 2006 Hard pp. 105

The Lake Fewa & a Horse
Poems New
Yuyutsu R.D. Sharma
ISBN 81-85693-34-X 2005 Paper pp. 108

Muna Madan
A Play in the Jhyaure Folk Tradition
Laxmi P. Devkota
Translated from the Nepali by **Anand P. Shrestha**
ISBN 81-85693-94-3 2000 pp.65

Where Laxmi Lies, Caged & other stories
Rajendra Yadav
Translated from the Hindi
ISBN 81-85693-86-2 2007 pp.125

Fever (Short Stories)
Sita Pandey
Translated from the Nepali
ISBN 81-85693-93-5 2001 Paper pp.96

Says Meera
An Anthology of Devotional Songs of Meera,
India's Greatest Woman Poet
Translated from the Hindi by **Vijay Munshi**
ISBN 81-85693-96-X 2001 Paper pp.76

Some Female Yeti & other Poems
Yuyutsu R.D.
ISBN 81-8250-010-9 2007 pp.68

In the City of Partridges (Poems)
Jagdish Chatturvedi
ISBN 81-85693-99-4 2004 Paper pp.90

Roaring Recitals: Five Nepali Poets
Gopal Prasad Rimal, Bhupi Sherchan, Shailendra & Others
Translated from the Nepali by
Yuyutsu R.D. Sharma
ISBN 81-85693-95-1 1999 Hard pp.99

Summer Rain
Three Decades of Poetry
K. Satchidanandan
ISBN 81-85693-90-0 1995 Paper pp.188

Sheet of Snow
An Anthology of Stories from the Himalayas
Translated from the Nepali by **Nagendra Sharma**
ISBN 81-85693-61-7 1997 paper pp.125

Dispossessed Nests: The 1984 Poems
Jayanta Mahapatra
ISBN 81-85693-74-9 1986 pp.69 Paper

To the Battlefield on an Elephant
Columns of Fire
Tara Nath Sharma
ISBN 81-85693-44-7 1999 pp.164 paper

The Change
A Novel based on the 1990 Democratic Upsurge in Nepal
Rishikeshab Raj Regmi
ISBN 81-85693-62-5 2001 pp.125

Blackout (A Novel) Tara Nath Sharma
Translated from the Nepali by **Larry Hartsell**
ISBN 81-85693-82-X 1990 pp.122

Elysium in the Halls of Hell
Poems about India **David Ray**
ISBN 81-85693-84-6 1991 pp.160

A Prayer in Daylight (Poems)
Yuyutsu R.D.
ISBN 81-85693-72-2 1984 paper pp.68

Hunger of Our Huddled Huts & Other Poems
Yuyutsu R.D.
ISBN 81-85693-80-3 2007 pp.65

Dying in Rajasthan (Short Stories)
Ramanand Rathi
ISBN 81-85693-71-4 1985 pp.62

The Black Sun (A Novel)
Bharat Jungam
ISBN 81-85693-84-6 1985 pp.78

IN NEPALI LANGUAGE

Panaharu Khalichan : Kavitaka Dui Dashak (Poems)
Yuyustu R.D. Sharma
Hard (Forthcoming)
ISBN 81-8250-004-4 2007 Paper pp. 102

Pashushala (Animal Farm) (A Novel)
Georege Orwell
Translated from the English by Bijuli Prasad Kayast
ISBN 81-8250-000-1 2004 Paper pp.96

Nepalko Prajatantrik Andolan Ko Itihas
Surya Mani Adhikary
ISBN 81-85693-54-4 1998 Paper pp.468

Geetajanjali (Nepali)
Rabindra Nath Tagore
Translated from the Bengali by **Ramesh Bhatta & Pashupati Neopane**
ISBN 81-85693-83-8 2000 Paper pp.125

Sarpahoru Geet Sundainan
Poems by **Shailendra Sakar**
ISBN 81-85693-97-8 1991 Hard pp.108